four seasons of poems
George Roberts

T A N K A Y E A R

DownStairs Press
Minneapolis, Minnesota
2015

DownStairs Press
Minneapolis, Minnesota
homewoodstudios.com/DownStairsPress

ISBN 978-0692644836

Cover photos by Jack Mader.

TANKA YEAR began with the gift of a workshop from my spouse, Beverly. Taught by Sheila Asato at the Minnesota Center for Book Arts, this two-day class on how to make book cloth from old kimonos was filled with historical and cultural information revealing the elaborate physical structure of the kimono, as well as its cultural, historical and aesthetic resonances. The results of the workshop, and several days of follow-up work in my studio, both surprised and pleased me, compelling me to consider a project worthy of such elegant fabric covers.

I set upon the idea of writing and printing a book of poetry. Tanka, a traditional Japanese verse form, like its brother haiku, carries some specific technical and content requirements ˜ ˜ thirty-one syllables, five lines, observation of nature, and reflection. My good friend, painter Mieko Yamazaki, explained, "tan", in Japanese, means short, and "ka" means poem or song. So a tanka year could be a collection of brief poems about the passage of time through the seasons. I eventually chose to write thirty-one poems for each of the four seasons, thus making a "tanka" of each season ˜ ˜ a suite of four books.

Most of these poems came to light in my back yard, or in my neighborhood, and were part of my daily habit of slowing down to notice how Monday was different from Sunday, how morning evolved into evening. Occasionally, as I was traveling, poems sprouted from other contexts. Subtexts identify those pages, and may help the reader. The original project, a letterpress printed edition of seven, sold immediately, and people began asking if the poems were available in another form.

Thus this standard edition, which attempts to echo the aesthetics of the hand-printed, deluxe edition, without encumbering either the printer (me) or the reader (you) with the time and cost a fine print edition requires. In the end, the poems carry the day. They are all here in this book for you to enjoy, I hope with the same spontaneous light in which they were written.

TANKA SPRING

pieces of moon fallen
from the Japanese cherry tree

one

dogged robin perched on the phone
wire, pushing her spring tunes
out into the cold blue sky
even while snow clings
to the withered grass

two

before green...hint of green
before leaves... sheathed buds nod,
the air shimmers, suggests
blossoms, fruit, harvests...
each day tumbles into the next

three

yesterday snow, flakes big as dreams
today a spray of yellow crocus
new maple leaf buds fountain
again this morning
red   red   red

four

late day sun drapes
sere and winter-worn sedum
in bronzed light   tiny blue
arctic squill sparkle   stars
against the warming earth

five

surprising spring hawk on the fence
white and gray feathers brushed with rust
head snapping here   then here
scouts the yard looking
for lunch

six

first night of thunder and rain
after a dark and snowy winter
the bright morning air
smells like the wrist
of a newborn baby

seven

lily-of-the-valley blooms
mason bees flit   ecstatic
we attend all winter
enduring the cold
for this scented moment

eight

constellation of surfers
stars   adrift in turquoise water
attending the right wave
to carry them
into emptiness

nine

in a pale dawn sky, white heron
wings west to cedar pond...
near dusk he flies east,
to the island in the river
trees full of nests

ten

purple beards loll in the sibilant breeze
a hundred pale blue iris nod
on supple green stems
butterflies
poised to take flight

eleven

silent blue horizon
here sea and sky change names
frigate birds ride the thermals
pulling invisible threads
through that thin blue line

twelve

jack-in-the-pulpits leap
and leaf out in the side yard
in less than a month...
newborns watching their hands
uncurling in the May light

thirteen

cardinal on the fence
puffed against the day-long rain
like us, shoulders hunched
hoping to avoid inevitable
raindrops

fourteen

flock of stars   heartbeats
tossed across the velvet sky
tiny white flowers...
light shower sparking dark waves
caressing the shore below

st. thomas, u.s. virgin islands

fifteen

before sunrise...   gray sky
hint of rose feathers the east
trees, leafed out and still...
the moment before language
fell into the world

sixteen

dianthus perfume dizzies the air
lifts color from its petals
weds it to our eyes...
so much in this world
without a body

seventeen

scarlet poppies lean
on lissome green stalks
toward the late afternoon sun...
an old man bent over,
asleep in dreams of his youth

eighteen

above a darkening lake
white heron pushed awry
by tumbling clouds...
at the rookery, chicks
gawp at the empty sky

nineteen

a bird whose name I do not know
scrapes her song
against the morning light...
pieces of moon fallen
from the japanese cherry tree

twenty

pearl mist enfolds nine brown ducks
serene as the morning light...
the water a wet gray cloud
below, webby feet churning
like engines

twenty-one

taupe dove, round buddha bird
serene on the power line,
your plaintive murmur
caressing the sunlit air...
waves kissing the wet shore below

twenty-two

late moon settles into the sea
sun not yet murmuring
islands rise from their silence...
ghosts of some distant time
with no need of us

st. thomas, u.s. virgin islands

twenty-three

as rainclouds part
the late sun dawdles
in the passionfruit vine...
a tiny cicada begins a song
she will sing through the night

twenty-four

sky goes dark　　the air cools
shots of hail brattle off the roof
then...　　sun returns
and like our mistakes and misgivings
everything calms

twenty-five

lull spider   blue as night
graced with yellow stripes
and silent as a secret, hangs
upside down in her web...
we speak the same language

twenty-six

slate clouds cloak the sky
inside the wind a tumbler falls
owls find their voices as dusk marks
late sun going down red
and red again

twenty-seven

lilies near the gallery window...
white sails on green reedy stems
curved to catch the wind...
paintings on the walls
gliding through the light

twenty-eight

bisque-toned lady cardinal
her roseate tail flicking
visits the serviceberry tree...
head snapping about
awaiting fruit

twenty-nine

saw-toothed lightning leaps   again
again white anemones in the garden
flash...
through all its darkness the heart attends
this luminous gift

thirty

after night   before morning...
blue   but not a color
a whisper   smoke hovers
then cloud   then island   then sky
and a kiss of rouge

st. thomas, u.s. virgin islands

thirty-one

the hush before summer
everything wild to grow...
flowers, trees, even language
sprouting astonished green tips
at the end of words

TANKA SUMMER

full moon walking across the sky

one

white berry tree petals
litter the grass...
spring departing already?
soon robins and cardinals
drunk on drops of tart red fruit

two

single crow, winter's court jester
barks in the alley...
where are your randy pals?
do leafed out trees mute
their sense of winter's farce?

three

in early morning spring drifts
into summer   dawn light bends,
almost says its name...
a longing comes over us
tongue-tied but welcome

four

silent white egret
knee deep in his own reflection...
I stand at the edge of Cedar Lake
watching the clouds
drifting beneath me

five

tranquil dragonfly still
on a green anemone stem...
blue body shimmering,
crystal wings drying
in the ardent morning sun

six

blue-black silence lingering...
trees dark and swaying...
above   river of stars
enfolds the deepening night
in its gauzy mantle

seven

wave of white anemone blossoms...
petals folding as darkness falls
reedlike stems reach up
supplicants
of the glowing moon

eight

creamy morning air floats
from daffodils to solitude
from pale pearl light
to whorling sky...
an infant learning to roll over

nine

dawn light dapples
through leafy elms   a single
cardinal pauses on a wire
then   frenzy of red
as the bird leaps free

ten

wildflowers along roadside swales
strewn like flung paint...
wheat grass enshrouded
in raspberry haze...
sun-struck insects flare then fade

bayfield, wisconsin

eleven

far out in the night,
bright beads drift like perfume...
below, dew settles
onto leaves of lily plants...
at sunrise, a necklace of stars!

twelve

long after the peonies idle, cut
from their roots and arranged
in a blue vase,
their scent bathes the room...
a distant singing of bells

thirteen

stark red cardinal, pale brown wings,
in the vee of a heavy oak branch...
perfectly still...
looking silently up
at the mute blue sky

fourteen

anemone petals fall, white
pages of a love story
torn, dropped...
late stars, early dew
holding off the inevitable

fifteen

on the kitchen screen, tiny dragonfly
black with gossamer wings
lingers to taste the sun   then
the angle of light wanes and...
gone

sixteen

blue vase on the kitchen table...
no breeze enters the house
yet blush petals fall,
the way we all must,
in amazed silence

seventeen

lissome, susurrous wings...   branches
of a great white pine across the street
flourish and bow in the wind...
monks nodding
at their simple prayers

eighteen

one fragile pink petal clings
to the drooping poppy...
has this moment of summer
passed so quickly?
where are the raspberries?

nineteen

two cardinals on the redwood fence
taupe mother tranquil, intent...
beige child, head flicking
rouge tail bobbing   eyes darting...
so much to learn

twenty

late night   dark sky   still
sifts phrases of deepest blue...
full moon walks across the night
refusing to forget
all who went before

twenty-one

gray heron wings
over glass-smooth Cedar Lake...
nor water nor bird attend
this ghostly reflection...
only the watcher on the shore

twenty-two

dark blue pollen beetle
plunders the indigo center
of a coral poppy...
clouds afloat overhead
mirrored on her back

twenty-three

stunned   even before thunder cracks
trees leap from the dark
again   and again lightning
sparks and flares...
giving them reason to quail

twenty-four

after rain   silent robin in the grass
head aslant   listening
to thought not yet a song ...
noisy worm munching
the dirt below

twenty-five

August sun sears the air
glinting off the sprinkler's shower...
monarch dawdles in the splash
forsaking sweet nectar
in favor of the dance

twenty-six

cardinal pair in the great red oak
crimson he, roseate she
tails flouncing   they flit inside
the branches...   here, then here
then not

twenty-seven

all morning   steady showers...
beneath the weight of water
dahlia and shrub rose droop
maple branches bend
...I bow with them

twenty-eight

after indulgent summer rain
glassy drops cling
to each nodding blade of grass
singing their songs of grief
singing their psalms of joy

twenty-nine

early morning sun seeps
through trees   between houses
the yard quiet, unmoving...
robins vigilant
not yet launching into song

thirty

blurred by vagabond mist
the island lingers,
distant and orphic,
across the steely blue water...
stories of our mother's youth

thirty-one

wind rustles dusty oak leaves
clouds meander through darkening skies,
waning quarter moon
shadows the heron's late flight
home to her nest

TANKA AUTUMN

October moon silvers the water

one

autumn sidles up out of the earth...
morning mist scrolls around the grass...
silence cradles everything...
a mother
outside of time

two

tiny blue dragonfly
wings invisible
alight on a tomato vine,
how to you live with such sapphire
light surrounding you?

three

undulate and color-rich hills
glide past the car window...
a Thomas Cole painting
unfurling itself
before and after us

gaspé peninsula, québec, canada

four

moss green grasshopper
leads me to the garden
while dew still lights the lawn...
little one, first I have seen,
where are you going so fast?

five

at dawn and again near dusk
elfin hummingbirds dart
from salvia to lupine...
the space between body
and want, all there is

six

thin rags of mist hang
above silver-still Wirth Lake...
heron flies, wide-winged, toward me,
settles near the cattail reeds,
takes up his vigil

seven

under jack-in-the-pulpit leaves
crimson berries spangle,
hold their own, bright as stars,
against the cooling sky...
and ask nothing of us

eight

stranger moon bathed amber
in smoke from Alberta forest fires...
wandering the dark sky...
lost child, waiting
to hear her name called out

nine

stinging nettles, poking up
among the tomatoes,
teach us to embrace
even the unpleasant parts
of our own blossoming

ten

chubby little house wren
balanced on a looping phone wire...
fearless   her hollow bones
sonorous in the golden
autumn light

eleven

late night of steady rain
dawn moon glows pale white
the sedum gone deep pink...
silent robins patrol the yard
listening for earthworms

twelve

not even the carking jay
raking his scratchy blue voice
against the dawn sky
can unsettle the calm
cloaking the dew-rinsed yard

thirteen

in Wirth Park meadow, a spatter
of burred milkweed pods yawning...
silken seed threads long adrift...
butterflies on their way
to Mexico

fourteen

opal evening sky pebbled
with flamingo clouds
lit from below by the sinking sun...
by a stream in the woods
ladyslippers nod

fifteen

rust-yellow patches dapple
lily-of-the-valley leaves...
mid-August sky, still blue
squirrels, still rash...
what solitude awaits us?

sixteen

sunlight skims through turning trees
crooks the air a dusty gold...
nights cool, wind grows brittle...
fallen leaves scuttle
toward eternity

seventeen

the night sky, endless...
nests in the oak trees, empty...
across the street, upstairs
one lamp burns in my friend's house...
he is likely reading

eighteen

sedum fall blush ripens...
frenzied by cooler nights,
steel blue mason bees dive
into smoke rose blossoms,
dream of sequestered eggs

nineteen

golden dawn light
fills with flute song...
one lark's voice joins another...
in time the raking of crows
will replace this autumn aubade

twenty

hosta withers and fades, lilies too...
the rose-pink heart
of the potted anthurium,
outside for summer.
bursts with winsome song

twenty-one

gray sandhill cranes tarry
at river's edge...
he, red crown aloft, eyes us...
she, nudges algae with her beak.
looking for clear water

sparta-elroy bike trail, southeast wisconsin

twenty-two

gauzy clouds drift down
creamy fog nestling
into orange-red maple branches...
cool morning air   so still
it could be memory

twenty-three

serene blue morning sky ...
paperwhite half moon
above fading willow...
fronds swaying in the breeze
spearpoint gold leaves everywhere

twenty-four

I turn, gaze back
at the path through Wirth Park...
three days of rain,
too late for oxeye daisies
already bending toward winter

twenty-five

petals drop from wilting
coneflowers   words fall
onto the page   mimesis...
but which is poetry?
and which the natural world?

twenty-six

the dusty air   indolent...
as if they had wings,
cricket trills flutter
through the turning trees...
leaves drop wordlessly to the ground

twenty-seven

poised on a fading cattail reed
warrior redwing blackbird
defending your domain,
don't you know
your fledglings have already left?

twenty-eight

stroll over Bassett Creek footbridge
at four in the morning ...
October moon silvers the water...
no one on the path,
anywhere

twenty-nine

a blind and blue light hovers
in the fragile seam
between October and winter...
the tongue-tied air turns
everything transparent

thirty

frogs' evening chorus   less rowdy,
the eddies where Bassett Creek flows
into Wirth Lake   less purling...
resolve to live
as an older man

thirty-one

a net of crows unfurls
above the roofs...
hints of snow in their loose silence...
their wing beats   a passage
to the sacred world

TANKA WINTER

light dropping from the moon
on newfallen snow

one

tufts of window frost
    skeletons of tiny birds
    fossiled by the icy air
linger above a forest
of crystal fern

two

a few withered leaves
cling   to the crabapple tree...
first snow of the season
wanders in like a vagabond
looking for work

three

black and barren linden branches
stretch their arms toward more light...
at sunrise   rose clouds
fuddle the snowy ground
in a pinkish glow

four

do you long to know how light feels
dropping from the canted moon
onto newfallen snow?
touch the unruffled cheek
of the one you love

five

I rummage through the gray morning
of memory...
then tingle
as a fleet frisson of snow
brattles against the frosted window

six

dark elm branches stretch
toward even darker night...
no stars   grandma's rough hands
crushing pecans with the handle
of a white kitchen knife

seven

moon and dog star snail
across the suede-blue night...
finespun phrases of gilded snowflakes
tremble on darkened tree limbs...
the heart's birthspace

eight

spartan raspberry stalks
poke through layers of earlier storms...
fresh, wind-bruised snow
mounds up against
an indifferent garage wall

nine

beneath dark clouds   a scattering
of light glints off snowy yards...
above these clouds   the stars
still wander
across the blanket of night

ten

leafless elm trees dark, still
new snow draping the tops
of their branches...   this silence,
could it be the moment
just before being born?

eleven

in the velvet blue light
before dawn   stars flare...
wet matches struck against
the harsh flint of endless space...
hints of pine sap tease the air

twelve

overnight   private snow
revealed by rabbit prints
close to the house...
edgy crows crayon the morning sky
with their rowdy banter

thirteen

sleepwalker moon lies down
on winter's shimmering quilt...
enfolds the clear night in her arms,
crooning the oldest lullaby
she knows

fourteen

spent and brittle fronds
from a neighbor's willow tree
stray   derelict   into our yard...
cryptic alphabet
of winter's cold brooding

fifteen

cloudless sky spills blue sunlight
onto fields of patient snow...
at night, pale thirsty moon
drinks reclusive light
from the shadowy drifts

sixteen

midnight blue evening...
cobalt blue morning...
serene new snow
luminous as a line of Li Po's verse
dusts the wooden porch railing

seventeen

frosty smoke drifts from chimneys...
tangerine dawn in the trees...
cornflower blue bowl of sky tips east...
and burnished day
breaks into bloom

eighteen

faint winds stir idle swings
in snowswept Farwell Park...
sentry streetlights kindle the drifts...
inside the silent houses   everyone
sleeping

nineteen

wise and bawdy crows, feathers ruffled
in raucous discourse...
confusion of clouds and fog
gives way to pliant ribbons
of blue winter light

twenty

wan slip of winter moon   there
bare oak branches   here
scudding clouds slink between...
wind swirls snow crystals
across the glassy ice on Wirth Lake

twenty-one

behind a cloak of muzzy clouds
an anemic sun, thumb-worn nickel,
rolls, without friends,
toward a darker corner
of the falling night

twenty-two

deep   bone cold   dark sky,
sleepy crescent moon leaning back...
opaque Japanese teacup
urging cherry blossoms
toward early spring

twenty-three

on her shimmering breath
lemon pale moon strays
across the star-quilted darkness...
feathery crystal light
finespun as a child's voice

twenty-four

near a neighbor's chimney ~ ~
huddled squirrel,
contemplating the hypnotic cold
with zenlike absence of concern...
gray smoke   gray sky

twenty-five

deep in the Wirth Park woods
a synod of rimed chokecherries,
rucked by winter's long breath,
clings to thin stalks...
patient, ruby musing

twenty-six

clouds dawdle, muffle the morning...
a haiku of snow dusts the yard...
a lone owl ask who?
by noon the sun breaks through
to read the poem

twenty-seven

whirling streamers of snow at noon...
crows descend from dark treetops...
later, a more docile snowfall...
by nighttime   silence,
and crow tracks

twenty-eight

days of long-awaited thaw...
then   more storms threaten...
still the persistent pump, hope,
throbs in the darkness
beneath the forgiving snow

twenty-nine

a wind-worked well of hip deep snow
skirts the maple tree...
distant push of iris bulbs...
the undaunted sun
reaching higher each day

thirty

late winter night   train cars slam
in the railyards near Wirth Park...
nor sleeping fox nor nodding owl stirs...
stoic drifts keep
their moonlit secrets

thirty-one

vast, cold, cryptic night...
stars close enough to touch...
distance blurs   then ceases to exist...
how much we are a part
of everything else

TANKA YEAR, a suite of poems in the Japanese style, was originally designed and printed in a fine press edition of seven at DownStairs Press in Garamond and Goudy Hand Tooled typefaces on Thai Mulberry paper with poems by George Roberts. Handmade book covers of kimono silk.

The standard edition, set in Garamond and Goudy Hand Tooled, was typeset by The Roberts Group and is printed on demand via CreateSpace.

www.ingramcontent.com/pod-product-compliance
Lightning Source LLC
LaVergne TN
LVHW011243080426
835509LV00005B/609